Anton Edelmann
Summer and Winter Casseroles

ANTON EDELMANN

Summer and Winter Casseroles

Photography by Philip Wilkins

WEIDENFELD & NICOLSON

Anton Edelmann

Anton Edelmann was born in Germany, where he began his training as a chef. His route to the top of his profession followed traditional culinary disciplines in some of the top hotel kitchens in Germany and London.

In 1982 Anton fulfilled his ambition to head the kitchen in one of the world's most fabled hotels, The Savoy. Here, with a brigade of 85 chefs, he is responsible for all meals served in the highly regarded River Restaurant, three banqueting rooms and eight private dining rooms. "We do not have freezers, nor do we have tin openers, because we do not need them. We work with fresh produce that arrives every morning – all £20,000 worth – which is prepared, cooked and served before the kitchen is cleared of food again the same night."

Anton Edelmann's first publication, *The Savoy Food and Drink Book*, marked The Savoy's centenary in 1989. Since then he has written several other books, including *Canapés and Frivolities, Creative Cuisine, Fast Feasts* and *Christmas Feasts*.

He has appeared in the BBC-TV series *Hot Chefs* and as a judge on *Masterchef*, and was a castaway on Radio 4's *Desert Island Discs* in April 1993. He lives in north London with his wife and their three daughters.

Contents

THE BASICS

Cooking

calls for a light head,

a generous spirit

and a large heart.

Introduction

A casserole is the name of both the cooking vessel and the dish cooked in it; the cooking method most frequently associated with casseroles is braising, slow cooking in a comparatively small amount of liquid. It is designed to tenderize the food, and it brings out the best in cuts of meat that would not respond well to quicker cooking techniques such as grilling or frying. However, braising need not be confined to meat: fish, poultry and vegetables such as red cabbage also respond well to this treatment.

A casserole or braised dish is perfect only if the sauce is well concentrated and all the flavours are intense. It requires an understanding of ingredients, and skill and care in the preparation. With a little patience you will achieve a culinary enlightenment.

I am a firm believer that cooking without herbs is like a language without grammar; they contribute a great deal to the basic structure of a dish, and also add a complementary colour and flavour when sprinkled liberally over a casserole just before serving.

Remember to be generous when you make a braised dish, as it often tastes even better when reheated.

BRAISED VEAL KNUCKLE

SERVES 4

1 veal knuckle, weighing
    about 2 kg/4½ lb
salt and pepper
25 g/1 oz unsalted butter
1½ tablespoons groundnut oil
1 large onion, chopped
2 carrots, chopped
1 stick of celery, chopped
1 leek, white and pale green
    parts only, chopped
2 garlic cloves, peeled and halved
200 g/7 oz ripe but firm plum
    tomatoes, skinned and
    seeded (reserve the skins
    and seeds), diced
50 g/2 oz tomato purée
250 ml/8 fl oz dry white wine
500 ml/16 fl oz chicken stock
½ teaspoon black peppercorns,
    lightly crushed
1 sprig of rosemary
1 sprig of thyme

Ask your butcher to trim off the meat, skin and gristle from the top 5 cm/2 inches of bone at the thin end of the knuckle. Trim the other end and season the meat. Preheat the oven to 180°/350°F/Gas Mark 4.

Heat a flameproof casserole just large enough to hold the knuckle comfortably. Add the butter and oil, then add the knuckle and brown it on all sides over moderate heat. Remove it from the pot. Add the onion, carrots, celery, leek and garlic to the casserole and cook until soft and lightly browned, stirring constantly. Stir in the tomato purée and the reserved tomato skins and seeds. Cook for 1 minute, stirring all the time. Stir a little of the wine into the vegetables and boil until evaporated. Add the remaining wine a little at a time and boil to evaporate, stirring frequently.

Return the knuckle to the casserole and add half the stock, the peppercorns and herbs. Cover and transfer to the oven for about 3 hours or until the meat is very tender and is falling off the bone. Turn the knuckle frequently during cooking and add the remaining stock a little at a time. Remove the lid for the last 20 minutes so the knuckle will have a good colour (check often, and add a little stock or water if necessary).

Remove the knuckle from the pot and keep warm. Strain the sauce through a sieve into a saucepan, pressing the vegetables. Bring to the boil, stir in the diced tomato, then taste and adjust the seasoning. Take the meat off the bone in one piece, slice it and serve hot, with the sauce.

Create a northern Italian-style menu with a first course salad of rocket with balsamic vinegar and Parmesan shavings and a dessert of sweet polenta with stewed fruit.

CHICKEN MOLE

SERVES 4

4 small chickens,
   about 1.1 kg/2½ lb each
1 onion, chopped
3 tablespoons olive oil
2 garlic cloves, crushed
2 tablespoons unsweetened
   cocoa powder
1 tablespoon tomato purée
2 tablespoons ground cumin
1 teaspoon ground cinnamon
1 teaspoon ground coriander
½ teaspoon cayenne pepper
85 g/3 oz roasted peanuts
500 ml/16 fl oz chicken stock
salt and pepper
125 ml/4 fl oz dry white wine
coriander leaves to garnish

Ask your butcher to split the chickens along the backs, remove the backbone and flatten them (birds prepared in this way are often referred to as butterflied or spatchcocked).

In a small saucepan, sauté the onion in 1 tablespoon of the olive oil until translucent. Add the garlic and cook for a further minute. Stir in the cocoa powder, tomato purée, spices and peanuts and mix thoroughly. Add the stock, bring to the boil and simmer, uncovered, until reduced by half: this will take at least 20 minutes.

While the sauce is cooking, season the chickens with salt and pepper, then heat the remaining olive oil in a wide saucepan or sauté pan and brown the chickens on both sides. Remove from the pan and drain on paper towels.

Pour off the oil from the pan, pour in the white wine and stir to deglaze, loosening any sediment. Return the chickens to the pan. Purée the sauce in a liquidizer or food processor and pour it over the chickens. Bring to the boil, then cover and simmer gently until the chickens are tender, about 30 minutes. Taste and adjust the seasoning and serve hot, garnished with fresh coriander.

Inspired by a traditional Mexican dish, this casserole is good in summer, served with fresh peas and rice spiced with cinnamon and cloves. Begin with some large prawns, sprinkled with crumbled feta cheese and capers, and finish with crisp filo pastry tartlets filled with exotic fruits.

NAVARIN OF LAMB

SERVES 4

Preheat the oven to 180°C/350°F/Gas Mark 4.

8 pieces of lamb from the
middle neck, each weighing
about 85 g/3 oz
salt and pepper
3 tablespoons groundnut oil
1 large onion, roughly chopped
1 carrot, roughly chopped
5 garlic cloves, roughly chopped
1 leek, white and green parts
only, roughly chopped
50 g/2 oz tomato purée
300 ml/10 fl oz red wine
25 g/1 oz plain flour
750 ml/1¼ pints chicken stock
1 sprig of thyme
1 sprig of marjoram

Trim the lamb and season with salt and pepper. Heat
a flameproof casserole over high heat and add the oil.
Brown the lamb briskly on both sides. Remove and
set aside.

Add the vegetables to the casserole and cook over
moderately low heat until lightly browned, stirring
often. Add the tomato purée and cook for 30 seconds,
stirring well. Add one-third of the wine, stir well and
bring to the boil. Boil until reduced to a thick glaze.
Repeat with the remaining wine, adding it half at a time.

Add the flour and stir well for 1 minute, then gradually
stir in the stock. Bring to the boil, add the herbs and some
salt and pepper, then return the lamb to the casserole.
Cover and transfer to the oven. Braise for about 2 hours
or until the lamb is very tender, stirring occasionally.

Remove the pieces of lamb from the casserole and keep
warm. Strain the sauce through a fine sieve into a jug or
bowl, pressing the vegetables to extract the maximum
flavour and liquid. Taste and adjust the seasoning. Spoon
the sauce over the lamb and serve hot.

*Navarin of lamb is often made with young spring or early
summer vegetables, but this version can be made at any time of
year. I like to serve it with couscous and chargrilled vegetables.
I might begin with a cool crab and avocado salad and finish
the meal with a rich almond tart served with crème fraîche.*

CHILLED BRAISED HAKE AND SALMON WITH TARRAGON AND FENNEL

SERVES 4

2 fennel bulbs
85 g/3 oz butter
salt and pepper
50 g/2 oz shallots,
  finely chopped
1 garlic clove, crushed
400 g/14 oz hake fillet, skin
  and bones removed and cut
  into 4 cm/1½ inch cubes
400 g/14 oz salmon fillet, skin
  and bones removed and cut
  into 4 cm/1½ inch cubes
400 ml/14 fl oz dry white wine
¼ bunch of parsley,
  stalks reserved,
  leaves finely chopped
½ bunch of tarragon,
  stalks reserved,
  leaves finely chopped
300 ml/10 fl oz double cream
2 plum tomatoes, skinned,
  seeded and diced

Preheat the oven to 180°C/350°F/Gas Mark 4.

Peel off and discard the outside leaves of the fennel; cut the fennel into 5 mm/¼ inch thick slices. Heat a flameproof casserole, add 50 g/2 oz of the butter and the fennel and season with salt and pepper. Fry until lightly coloured on both sides, then remove with a slotted spoon.

Add a little more butter to the casserole, add the shallots and sweat over a low heat until soft and translucent. Add the garlic and sweat for a further minute. Add the fennel, fish, wine and parsley and tarragon stalks, cover and cook in the oven for about 10 minutes or until the fish is tender.

Using a slotted spoon, remove the fennel and fish to a plate, cover and cool until lukewarm.

Strain the liquid into a saucepan and boil over high heat until it thickens slightly, then add the cream and diced tomatoes and boil again until it reduces and thickens. Place the saucepan over ice and stir until cool.

Add the tarragon and parsley leaves and taste and adjust the seasoning. Place two slices of fennel on each plate, arrange the fish on top and pour the sauce over the fish.

A light casserole for early summer, accompanied by new potatoes and mangetout. For a first course, I suggest a salad of slender leeks and quails' eggs, and as a light dessert, perhaps some seasonal fruit tumbling over a mound of quark or ricotta cheese.

BRAISED MONKFISH IN RED WINE

SERVES 4

Preheat the oven to 160°/325°/Gas Mark 3.

125 g/4 oz small button
onions, peeled
3 tablespoons vegetable oil
250 g/9 oz unsalted butter,
cut into cubes
125 g/4 oz small button
mushrooms
salt and pepper
85 g/3 oz smoked streaky bacon
675 g/1½ lb monkfish fillets,
trimmed and cut into
12 equal pieces
50 g/2 oz shallots, finely
chopped
200 ml/7 fl oz chicken stock
600 ml/1 pint red wine
4 tablespoons double cream
½ teaspoon redcurrant jelly
1 tablespoon chopped
fresh parsley

Place the button onions in a saucepan just large enough
to hold them in a single layer. Add a little oil and fry
over high heat until well coloured on all sides. Reduce
the heat, cover with a lid and cook slowly until soft.

Heat a little butter in a saucepan, add the mushrooms
and cook over high heat. Season with salt and pepper.

Grill the bacon on both sides until crisp. Cut into
1 cm/½ inch strips.

Season the fish. Heat a flameproof casserole, add a little
butter, then add the fish and fry until lightly coloured
on both sides. Remove the fish from the casserole, add
the shallots and cook until soft. Return the fish to the
casserole, add the stock and half the red wine, cover and
braise in the oven for about 30 minutes, until tender.

Using a slotted spoon, remove the fish to a warmed
plate, cover and keep warm.

Add the remaining wine to the casserole and boil over
high heat until it reduces and thickens. Add the cream
and reduce again. Remove from the heat and beat in
the butter and redcurrant jelly. Add the fish, onions
and mushrooms, then taste and adjust the seasoning.
Serve on warmed plates, sprinkled with the crisp bacon
and parsley.

Serve at any time of year, accompanied by saffron rice.
Begin the meal with a salad, perhaps of marinated vegetables.
Follow with a refreshing fruit dessert such as lemon sorbet.

BRAISED DUCK LEGS WITH CABBAGE

SERVES 4

8 duck legs
salt and pepper
500 ml/16 fl oz duck fat*
200 g/7 oz golden syrup
50 ml/2 fl oz dry white wine
300 ml/10 fl oz soy sauce
6 tablespoons sesame oil
2.5 cm/1 inch piece of fresh
  ginger, sliced
8 cloves
1 fresh red chilli, sliced
5 star aniseed
5 cardamom pods
5 coriander seeds
1 teaspoon Chinese five-spice
  powder
50 g/2 oz garlic,
  very thinly sliced
1 kg/2¼ lb Chinese cabbage,
  large stalks removed
3 tablespoons vegetable oil
50 g/2 oz sugar
125 ml/4 fl oz duck
  or chicken stock

* Whenever you cook duck,
strain off and reserve the fat.
It can be kept in the refrigerator
for up to 2 months, and is
delicious for other dishes,
such as sautéed potatoes.

Preheat the oven to 160°C/325°F/Gas Mark 3.

Season the duck legs and place in a flameproof casserole.
Add the duck fat, golden syrup, wine, 100 ml/3½ fl oz
of the soy sauce, 3 tablespoons of the sesame oil, the
spices and one-third of the garlic. Bring to the boil, then
place in the oven and simmer gently for 1½–2 hours,
until the legs are very tender.

Using a slotted spoon, transfer the legs to a baking sheet
and brown in the oven, basting occasionally with a little
of their cooking liquid. When they are browned, leave
to cool slightly, then trim 2 cm/¾ inch of the skin from
the top of the legs. Keep warm.

While the duck is browning, blanch the cabbage in
boiling salted water for 10 seconds. Refresh in iced
water and drain well. Heat the vegetable oil in a small
frying pan and fry the remaining garlic over a low heat
until golden brown. Remove and drain on paper towels.

Put the sugar in a small, heavy saucepan with 3 tablespoons water and cook over medium heat until it turns
golden brown. Then add 100 ml/3½ fl oz of the soy
sauce and the duck stock, and boil until syrupy.

Heat the remaining sesame oil in a large saucepan, add
the cabbage and the remaining soy sauce. When hot,
place the cabbage on four warmed plates, top with the
duck and drizzle a little of the sauce around it. Sprinkle
with the garlic crisps and serve hot.

*As an accompaniment, serve rösti potatoes. A scallop and
potato salad would make a good starter, with a simple rhubarb
compote for pudding.*

Rabbit with ginger, mustard and polenta

SERVES 4

1 rabbit
salt and pepper
4 tablespoons coarsegrain
   mustard
2 tablespoons plain flour
2 tablespoons groundnut oil
100 g/3½ oz unsalted butter
1 onion, finely chopped
1 garlic clove, crushed
1 teaspoon freshly grated ginger
2 tablespoons medium-sweet
   sherry
2 tablespoons tarragon vinegar
900 ml/1½ pints chicken stock
100 ml/3½ fl oz double cream
100 g/3½ oz polenta (coarse
   maize flour)
4 plum tomatoes, skinned,
   seeded and diced
2 tablespoons chopped
   fresh tarragon
85 g/3 oz taleggio cheese,
   cut into thin slices
8 fresh sage leaves, chopped

Ask your butcher to joint the rabbit so that you have 10 pieces: the legs cut in half, the saddle cut into four pieces and the shoulders.

Preheat the oven to 180°C/350°F/Gas Mark 4. Season the rabbit, then brush the mustard on generously and dust with the flour. Heat half the oil in a flameproof casserole; add the rabbit and 25 g/1 oz of the butter. Turn the rabbit until it is golden brown all over.

Remove the rabbit from the casserole and pour away the fat. Add the remaining butter and then the onion and sweat over a low heat until soft. Add the garlic and ginger and sweat for a further minute. Stir in the sherry and vinegar and boil over high heat until reduced by half. Add 400 ml/14 fl oz of the stock and boil until reduced by two-thirds. Add the cream and return the rabbit to the casserole. Cover with a lid and cook in the oven for about 30 minutes, until the meat is tender.

Meanwhile, heat the remaining stock in a saucepan, add the rest of the butter and stir in the polenta in a thin, steady stream, stirring continuously with a whisk so that no lumps form. Reduce the heat and stir frequently until the polenta starts to come away from the sides of the pan; this will take about 40 minutes.

Using a slotted spoon, remove the rabbit to a warmed plate. Boil the sauce until slightly thickened. At the last minute, add the tomatoes and tarragon and taste and adjust the seasoning. Add the butter, sage and cheese to the polenta and serve with the rabbit and its sauce.

Serve in spring or summer, preceded by a fish soup with aïoli and followed by a light orange dessert such as a cold soufflé.

LAMB PEPERONATA

SERVES 4

3 red peppers
3 yellow peppers
3 green peppers
1 aubergine
200 ml/7 fl oz extra virgin
    olive oil
2 onions, finely chopped
2 garlic cloves, finely chopped
3 plum tomatoes, skinned,
    seeded and diced
1 tablespoon tomato purée
200 ml/7 fl oz dry white wine
12 lamb cutlets, trimmed
200 ml/7 fl oz chicken
    or lamb stock
salt and pepper

Preheat the oven to 190°C/375°F/Gas Mark 5.

Grill the peppers until blackened and blistered on all sides. Transfer to a polythene bag and leave for 5 minutes or until cool enough to handle. Peel off the blackened skin, scrape out the seeds and cut the flesh into 1 cm/½ inch strips. Cut the aubergine lengthways into 1 cm/½ inch slices, then cut into strips similar in size to the peppers.

Heat the olive oil in a large flameproof casserole, add the onions and sweat over a low heat until soft. Add the garlic and sweat for a further minute. Add the tomatoes and cook for 3–4 minutes, then add the tomato purée and cook for 2–3 minutes. Add the wine and boil over high heat until it is reduced by half. Add the peppers and aubergine strips and stir to mix, then add the lamb cutlets and cover with the pepper mixture. Pour in the stock and season generously. Bring back to a simmer, then transfer to the oven and braise, uncovered, for 45–60 minutes, stirring occasionally, until the meat is tender. Taste and adjust the seasoning and serve hot.

Serve with a potato purée flavoured with good olive oil. For a first course I suggest a smoked haddock chowder with grilled bacon. To finish, how about pears with butterscotch sauce?

PHEASANT WITH SAUERKRAUT

SERVES 4

85 g/3 oz smoked streaky
    bacon rashers
3 tablespoons groundnut oil
1 onion, thinly sliced
450 g/1 lb sauerkraut, washed
    well in cold water and drained
100 ml/3½ fl oz dry white wine
200 ml/7 fl oz chicken stock
½ bay leaf
2 juniper berries
2 large carrots
2 oven-ready pheasants
salt and pepper
200 g/7 oz garlic sausage

Preheat the oven to 200°C/400°F/Gas Mark 6.

Put the bacon in a saucepan of cold water, bring to the boil and simmer for 10 minutes. Drain and refresh in cold water.

Heat a little of the oil in a flameproof casserole, add the onion and sweat over low heat until soft and translucent. Add the sauerkraut, wine, stock, bay leaf, juniper berries, carrots and bacon. Bring to the boil, cover with a lid and cook in the oven for 1 hour, stirring frequently.

Season the pheasants inside and out with salt and pepper. Heat the remaining oil in a roasting tin and turn the pheasants in the hot oil. Lay them on one side and roast in the hot oven for 5 minutes. Turn them over on to the other side and roast for 5 minutes, then turn them on to their backs and roast for a further 5 minutes. Remove from the oven and leave to cool slightly.

Cut each pheasant in half and remove the bones. Place them in the casserole with the sauerkraut, add the garlic sausage, cover with the lid and return to the oven for another 30 minutes.

Remove from the oven and season the sauerkraut to taste. Remove the rind from the bacon and cut into slices. Remove the skin from the garlic sausage and cut into slices. Slice the carrots. Arrange the pheasants with the sauerkraut, bacon and garlic sausage on four warmed plates and garnish with the carrots.

Serve this autumn casserole with a purée of cauliflower and potatoes, and follow with lemon pancakes with vanilla ice cream.

Sweet and sour braised beef

SERVES 4–6

1 leek, sliced
2 carrots, sliced
2 sticks of celery, sliced
3 onions, sliced
250 ml/8 fl oz red wine
250 ml/8 fl oz red wine vinegar
1.5 kg/3 lb kg chuck of beef,
   in one piece
½ bunch parsley
salt and pepper
3 tablespoons vegetable oil
1 bay leaf
2 cloves
4 juniper berries, crushed
½ teaspoon black peppercorns,
   crushed
2 tablespoons raisins
100 g/3½ oz unsalted butter,
   cut into cubes

Put the vegetables, wine and vinegar in a saucepan, bring to the boil and then leave to cool. Place the meat in a large bowl, pour on the vegetable mixture and its liquid and add the parsley. Cover and leave in the refrigerator to marinate for at least 48 hours (the longer you leave it in the marinade the more tender the meat becomes).

Preheat the oven to 160°C/325°F/Gas Mark 3.

Remove the meat from the marinade, pat dry and season with salt and pepper. Heat the oil in a flameproof casserole over high heat, add the meat and brown well on all sides. Pour in enough of the marinade to half cover the meat. Wrap the bay leaf, cloves, juniper berries and peppercorns in a piece of muslin and add to the casserole. Cook in the oven for about 3 hours, adding more marinade if necessary, until the meat is tender.

Remove the meat from the liquid, wrap in foil and keep warm. Press the liquid through a fine sieve into a saucepan and boil until it thickens slightly. Add the raisins and whisk in the butter. Slice the meat and pour over the sauce. Serve hot.

Serve with braised red cabbage and dumplings. A fresh-looking first course might be grilled asparagus with Parma ham, followed by a fresh-tasting pudding such as lemon posset.

RICH BEEF CASSEROLE

SERVES 4

1 kg/2¼ lb boneless beef such
 as brisket or chuck, trimmed
 and cut into 5 cm/2 inch
 cubes
150 g/5 oz button mushrooms,
 quartered if large
2 onions, thickly sliced
2 carrots, thickly sliced
2 sticks of celery, thickly sliced
1 large leek, white and pale
 green parts only, sliced
3 garlic cloves, peeled
1 bottle of red wine
salt and pepper
flour for coating
100 ml/3½ fl oz vegetable oil
25 g/1 oz unsalted butter
100 g/3½ oz tomato purée
500 ml/16 fl oz chicken stock
3 sprigs of thyme
1 bay leaf

Place the beef in a large bowl with the vegetables and
garlic and add the wine. Cover and leave to marinate in
the refrigerator for 2 days.

Drain the meat and vegetables in a colander set over a
bowl. Reserve the marinating liquid. Separate the beef,
vegetables and mushrooms. Preheat the oven to 150°C/
300°F/Gas Mark 2.

Pat the beef dry with paper towels. Season, then coat
lightly with flour. Heat a flameproof casserole over high
heat and add enough oil to make a film on the bottom.
Fry the cubes of beef, a few at a time, until well
browned. When all the beef has been browned and
removed from the casserole, pour off the fat.

Add a little more oil to the casserole with half the butter
and reduce the heat to moderate. Cook the marinated
vegetables and garlic until soft and lightly browned,
stirring often. Stir in the tomato purée. Add a ladleful of
the marinating liquid and bring to the boil. Boil until
reduced to a glaze. Add another ladleful of the liquid
and boil to reduce again. Continue adding the liquid
little by little. When all the liquid has been added and
reduced, stir in the stock and bring to the boil. Return
the beef to the casserole and add the herbs. Cover and
transfer to the oven. Cook for 2½−3 hours or until the
beef is very tender, stirring frequently.

To serve, sauté the reserved mushrooms in butter. Reheat
the casserole if necessary and serve with the mushrooms.

*Serve with vegetables roasted in olive oil. Roast for the
following times: corn on the cob and whole garlic bulbs 50
minutes; celeriac 45 minutes; carrots 40 minutes; cauliflower
35 minutes; parsnips 30 minutes.*

BRAISED OXTAIL ON CELERIAC PURÉE

SERVES 6

2 boned oxtails (ask your
    butcher to do this)
salt and pepper
2 bay leaves
2 sage leaves
2 tablespoons vegetable oil
1 carrot, chopped
1 onion, chopped
200 ml/7 fl oz red wine
100 ml/3½ fl oz Madeira
500 ml/16 fl oz chicken stock
500 g/1 lb 2 oz celeriac,
    peeled and cubed
150 ml/5 fl oz milk
50 g/2 oz chilled unsalted butter
2 tablespoons chopped
    fresh parsley

Preheat the oven to 200°C/400°F/Gas Mark 6.

Season the oxtails with salt and pepper. Place the bay and sage leaves on one oxtail and then place the other one on top, with the wide ends over the thin ends. Fold over both end pieces, roll into a round shape and tie with kitchen string.

Heat the oil in a flameproof casserole and fry the meat until well browned on all sides. Discard the oil and add the vegetables, wine, Madeira and stock to cover the meat. Cover with a lid and cook in the oven for 3½ hours, until the meat is really tender. Remove the meat, discard the string and wrap tightly in cling film. Cool, then chill.

Boil the liquid to reduce by two-thirds, then pass through a fine sieve into a saucepan.

Cook the celeriac in the milk with a little salt and pepper until very soft. Pour away two-thirds of the milk, then purée the remaining milk and celeriac and stir in a little of the butter. Season to taste and keep warm.

Cut the oxtail, in the cling film, into 5 cm/2 inch slices. Wrap each slice in fresh cling film. Reheat over steam.

Meanwhile, reheat the sauce and whisk in the remaining butter. Season to taste. Put some celeriac purée on four warmed plates. Remove the cling film from the oxtail and arrange on the celeriac. Pour over the sauce and sprinkle with the chopped parsley.

Some crisp boiled green beans would be the ideal accompaniment. Begin the meal with Caesar salad, and finish with apple tart and cinnamon cream.

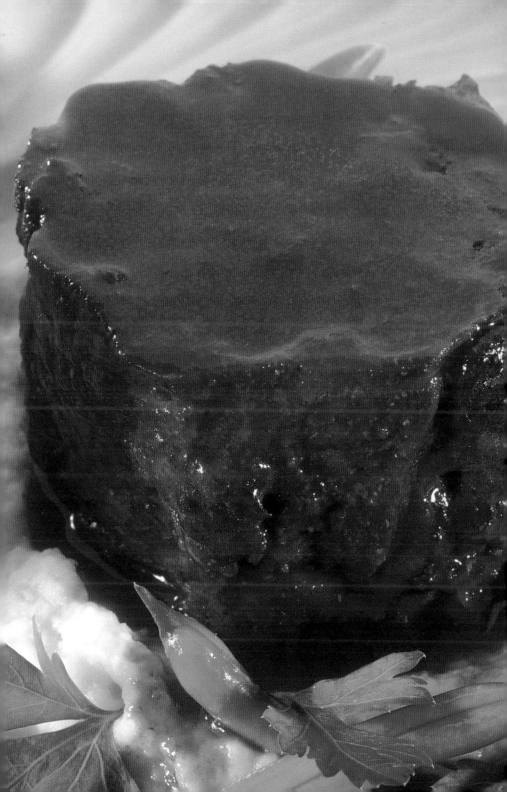

The Basics

CASSEROLE INGREDIENTS

Braising brings out the best in cuts of meat that have a high percentage of muscle tissue and a good covering or marbling of fat that will melt and 'baste' the meat throughout the slow cooking process, keeping it moist and succulent.

If you use a lean joint you should first lard the meat with small strips of pork fat: cut the pork fat into pieces approximately 2 x 1 cm/1 x ½ inch and use a larding needle to insert it along the grain of the meat (you could ask your butcher to do this for you).

Poultry and game birds can be braised whole or cut into pieces. If you braise them whole, cover the breast with bacon to stop them from drying out during the cooking process.

IDEAL JOINTS
FOR BRAISING
AND CASSEROLES

Lamb: neck, shoulder, rump

Veal: shin, cushion, best end, silverside, sweetbreads

Beef: rump, brisket, cheek, topside, chuck, oxtail

Pork: neck, knuckle, shoulder, belly, head

Poultry and game: all poultry, game birds, rabbits, hare and haunch of venison

Fish: hake, monkfish, salmon, turbot

STOCK

It is obviously best to use the appropriate stock – veal stock for braising veal, fish stock for braising fish etc. – but this is not always easy in a domestic environment. Instead, I suggest that you use a good chicken stock, which is amazingly versatile. It takes on other flavours very easily and helps to intensify them.

MARINADES

Larger pieces of meat benefit from being marinated, either in wine or vinegar, which help to tenderize the muscle. For the wine, I suggest you use a good-quality table wine for cooking and keep the Château Lafite to drink with the meal.

Fish and poultry do not need this tenderizing process, and a marinade to add exotic flavours such as ginger, soy sauce, garam masala or lemongrass would be more appropriate.

EQUIPMENT

The casserole or pot for braising in should be just large enough to hold the joint or pieces snugly and must have a well-fitting lid.

BRAISING TIPS AND TECHNIQUES

First season the meat well. Heat the casserole, then add oil or half oil and half butter and when the fat is hot, add the meat and seal it in the fat until well coloured. Remove the meat from the casserole.

Add the vegetables and brown lightly. A crucial stage in braising meat is when you add the tomato purée to the vegetables, then the wine and/or stock; this should result in a deep colour and silky, glossy sauce. The colour begins to deepen when you caramelize the tomato purée. Then you gradually add small amounts of wine or stock and let them evaporate before adding more. Every time the liquid reduces, it gets darker; this usually has to be done three or four times. This also thickens the braising liquid.

You then return the meat or poultry to the casserole and pour in wine or stock no higher than a quarter of the way up the main ingredient, cover and place in the oven.

Braising must take place at a low temperature, approximately 180°C/350°F/Gas Mark 4, in order for the meat to become very tender. The slower the cooking process the better the result. If you braise too quickly, at too high a temperature, the meat will become stringy and dry. Baste and turn the meat frequently and if the sauce is drying up, top it up with some more stock.

For the last 30 minutes cooking time, remove the lid so the meat takes on some colour. With the lid off, the liquid evaporates more quickly, so make sure that you stir often and add wine or stock when necessary.

Once it is very tender, remove the meat and keep warm. Pass the sauce through a fine sieve and push through the vegetables, which add to the flavour and help to thicken the sauce.

Classic Cooking

STARTERS

Lesley Waters A former chef and now a popular television cook, appearing regularly on *Ready Steady Cook* and *Can't Cook Won't Cook*. Author of several cookery books.

VEGETABLE SOUPS

Elisabeth Luard Cookery writer for the *Sunday Telegraph Magazine* and author of *European Peasant Food* and *European Festival Food*, which won a Glenfiddich Award.

GOURMET SALADS

Sonia Stevenson The first woman chef in the UK to be awarded a Michelin star at the Horn of Plenty in Devon. Author of *The Magic of Saucery* and *Fresh Ways with Fish*.

FISH AND SHELLFISH

Gordon Ramsay Chef/proprietor of London's Aubergine restaurant, recently awarded its second Michelin star, and author of Glenfiddich Award-winning *A Passion for Flavour*.

CHICKEN, DUCK AND GAME

Nick Nairn Chef/patron of Braeval restaurant near Aberfoyle in Scotland, whose BBC-TV series *Wild Harvest* was last summer's most successful cookery series, accompanied by a book.

LIVERS, SWEETBREADS AND KIDNEYS

Simon Hopkinson Former chef/patron at London's Bibendum restaurant, columnist and author of *Roast Chicken and Other Stories* and *The Prawn Cocktail Years*.

VEGETARIAN

Rosamond Richardson Author of several vegetarian titles, including *The Great Green Cookbook* and *Food from Green Places*.

PASTA

Joy Davies One of the creators of *BBC Good Food Magazine*, she has been food editor of *She, Woman* and *Options* and written for the *Guardian, Daily Telegraph* and *Harpers & Queen*.

CHEESE DISHES

Rose Elliot The UK's most successful vegetarian cookery writer and author of many books, including *Not Just a Load of Old Lentils* and *The Classic Vegetarian Cookbook*.

POTATO DISHES

Patrick McDonald Former chef/patron of the acclaimed Epicurean restaurant in Cheltenham, and food consultant to Sir Rocco Forte Hotels.

BISTRO

Anne Willan Founder and director of La Varenne Cookery School in Burgundy and West Virginia. Author of many books and a specialist in French cuisine.

ITALIAN

Anna Del Conte Author of several books on Italian food, including *The Gastronomy of Italy*, *Secrets from an Italian Kitchen* and *The Classic Food of Northern Italy* (chosen as the 1996 Guild of Food Writers Book of the Year).

VIETNAMESE

Nicole Routhier One of the United States' most popular cookery writers, her books include *Cooking Under Wraps, Nicole Routhier's Fruit Cookbook* and the award-winning *The Foods of Vietnam*.

MALAYSIAN

Jill Dupleix One of Australia's best known cookery writers and broadcasters, with columns in the *Sydney Morning Herald* and *Elle*. Her books include *New Food* and *Allegro al dente*.

PEKING CUISINE

Helen Chen Author of *Chinese Home Cooking*, she learned to cook traditional Peking dishes from her mother, Joyce Chen, the *grande dame* of Chinese cooking in the United States.

STIR-FRIES

Kay Fairfax A writer and broadcaster whose books include *100 Great Stir-fries, Homemade* and *The Australian Christmas Book*.

NOODLES

Terry Durack Australia's most widely read restaurant critic and co-editor of the *Sydney Morning Herald Good Food Guide*. He is the author of *YUM*, a book of stories and recipes.

NORTH INDIAN CURRIES

Pat Chapman Founded the Curry Club in 1982. A regular broadcaster on television and radio, he is the author of 20 books, which have sold more than 1 million copies.

GRILLS AND BARBECUES

Brian Turner Chef/patron of Turner's in Knightsbridge and one of Britain's most popular food broadcasters; he appears frequently on *Ready Steady Cook, Food and Drink* and many other television programmes.

SUMMER AND WINTER CASSEROLES

Anton Edelmann Maître Chef des Cuisines at the Savoy Hotel, London. Author of six cookery books, he has also appeared on television.

TRADITIONAL PUDDINGS

Tessa Bramley Chef/patron of the acclaimed Old Vicarage restaurant in Ridgeway, Derbyshire and author of *The Instinctive Cook*.

DECORATED CAKES

Jane Asher Author of several cookery books and a novel. She has also appeared in her own television series, *Jane Asher's Christmas* (1995).

FAVOURITE CAKES

Mary Berry One of Britain's leading cookery writers, her numerous books include *Mary Berry's Ultimate Cake Book*. She has made many television and radio appearances.

ICE CREAMS AND SEMI FREDDI

Ann and Franco Taruschio Owners of the renowned Walnut Tree Inn near Abergavenny in Wales, soon to appear in a television series, *Franco and Friends: Food from the Walnut Tree*. They have written three books together.

Text © Anton Edelmann 1997

Anton Edelmann has asserted his right to be identified
as the author of this Work.

Photographs © Philip Wilkins 1997

First published in 1997 by
George Weidenfeld & Nicolson
The Orion Publishing Group
Orion House
5 Upper St Martin's Lane
London WC2H 9EA

British Library Cataloguing-in-Publication data
A catalogue record for this book is available from
the British Library

ISBN 0 297 82274 8

Designed by Lucy Holmes
Edited by Maggie Ramsay
Food styling by Louise Pickford
Typesetting by Tiger Typeset